Life As A Cycle

Life As A Cycle

Awakening
Love
Exploring
Spirit

Rosalie Jones

RXR Studios Research and Development

Contents

Contents

Contents

To Randolph Frank Sanchez. The living love of my life. I appreciate you everyday. Forever! You always remind me to live in the present moment. You said, " Seasons come, seasons go. The sun rises, the sun sets. On and on, the eternal flow. And one day the sun will rise and I won't be here anymore."

To my father Donald Walden Jones. Thank you for inspiring me to put this book together. Honest, encouraging, and supportive of all my creative interests. You have given me the best opportunities to be an authentic and empowered human being. I love you Daddy-O!

Awakening

Built Of Light

We are built of light my friends.
Created from bits of dust.
Pieced by chance.
An optical heat.
Each of us reside in our

own

spacious

holes

in the air.
Creating waves of energy.
Take heed the light
in which you dwell.
For what lies between
each dust speck
is eternal.

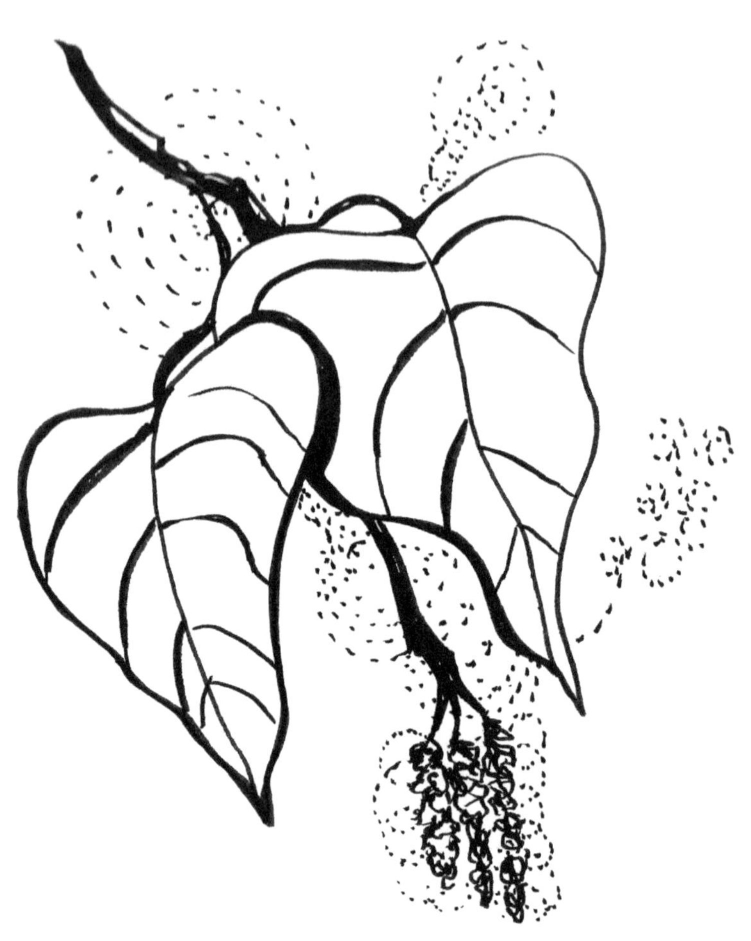

Cottonwood

What if we were born as seeds?
This life was just waiting
to crack open?
I saw a seed today
flying through the air.
Like us, nothing is random.
It's just the way it is.

Looking for paw prints on the the road.
A traveler before me, revealing itself.

Thunderheads and falling leaves.
Mullein torches in the field.

These are golden days.
Seeds are rolling in the wind.

Life is so touch and go.
When it looks like rain,
the fire cloud
rolls in again.

For Mom

If you were born smiling,
shining like your mother's face.
Your world is
beautiful.
Every step
yearning to embrace.

The world
you create.
Reflecting always
your mother's face.
Moments
come and go.
The moment I was born,
I shared a
light with you.

Many years into the future
we see our love grow.
A light that reaches across the world,
no matter where we go.

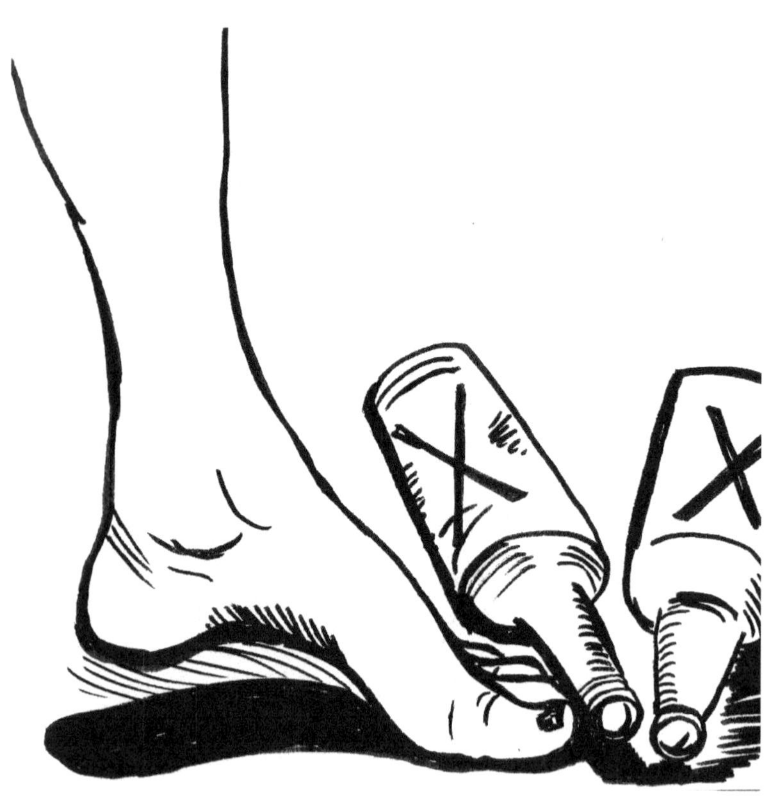

Breaking The chain

Nothing but gone.
Been poisoned for too long.
Nothing but gone.
When the drink took our reason.
Nothing but gone,
since they took this nation.

My family arrived on the Mayflower.
Into the wild
of a higher power.
Digging in, making space.
Polluting the future of the original race.
Generations come, generations go.
How we live today,
compared to long ago.

Bringing the streets of man
into the heart of gold.

Original is aboriginal.
I was a druid long ago.

Entitled

Is there a reason
so many
are pleading
for a new life?

When innocent
children
carry the weight
of every
mistake.

Everything
taken
and never
replaced.

Tree Of Life

The
universe
is
open
to
our
being.

She
cradles
us
with
branches.

Rooted
in
the
Tree
of
Life

{ 2 }

Love

Paradise

In your bed
on a beach.
Shooting stars,
feel the heat.

I'm romancing
with you.
I'm standing
with you.

On a crescent
beach.
A trinity of heat.
Fulfill
a wild child's
fantasy.

In your bed
on a beach.
My South Pacific
heart beat.

Ocean Blue

Into your eyes I fall again.
Come full circle
I feel the same.
Lovers here, and more have gone.
Turning space
relaying time.
A
baby lives
A
baby dies.
Through thick and thin
we have survived.
Into the deep
she'll carry you.
Exotic shores
wild and new.
It's hard to bear
though it was real.
Lasting love, drawing near.

Closer

Like a voiceless wind,
and a silent ocean,
these words cannot be spoken.
World's coming together
bring a voice
to my heart.
Love being reborn
from the original start.
Every time I speak,
words fall
to the ground.
Every time I step up,
reason tells me
to sit down.
I'll rise to the occasion
and say I love you.
A sound breaks the ice,
brings me closer
to the truth.

Rose

Silent movements,
rustling wind,
window open.

Remember scars.
Smelling times of
distant blooming.

Out the window,
through the thorns,
beyond the branches.

Arching into me.
A new rose to bloom.

Wave of rose,
crashing through
the window.

Wave of rose,
tearing through my heart.

Touching The Clouds

We fall in love
around the big drum.
Singing together
our heart song.

Raising them up,
a circle of voices.
Touching the clouds,
allowing deep focus.

Soul touching soul.
Knowing the deepest love.
From heart to heart,
and spark to spark.

A rhythm of
nations,
passion and
celebration.

Exploring

Traveler

The windows are open.
Praha sounds filter
into the room,
three stories tall.

Rain seeps
down the street.
Collecting
into rivulets of water
between
the cobblestones.

My heart beats.
The Locust trees.
Ivy crawls.

With pack, water,
and two
wandering feet,
I journey into
the rain soaked streets.

Castle Wall

Unwinding from a long night.
Celebrating until daylight.

Traveling up the castle wall,
up the river through the hall.

To see the river down below.
And watch the golden towers glow.

We watch the sunrise
above the streets of stone.

Looking into your eyes,
time has always been alone.

Life Is Taste

We
bring the seams
together.

Creating
our
personalities.

Wanderers
grow
holy roots.

Stretching
across
humanity.

Life is taste.

On the edge
of a parched
earth.

The Keys

Land of lightning,
people passages.
Mangrove tree,
one among many.

Larger than life,
given the space to grow.

Carve the stone.
Tap the chisel.
Bridges not bloodshed.

Dreaming a luxury,
by taxing the earth?

Like a cloud suspended
above the water.

White light reflecting
the following eyes
of a painting.

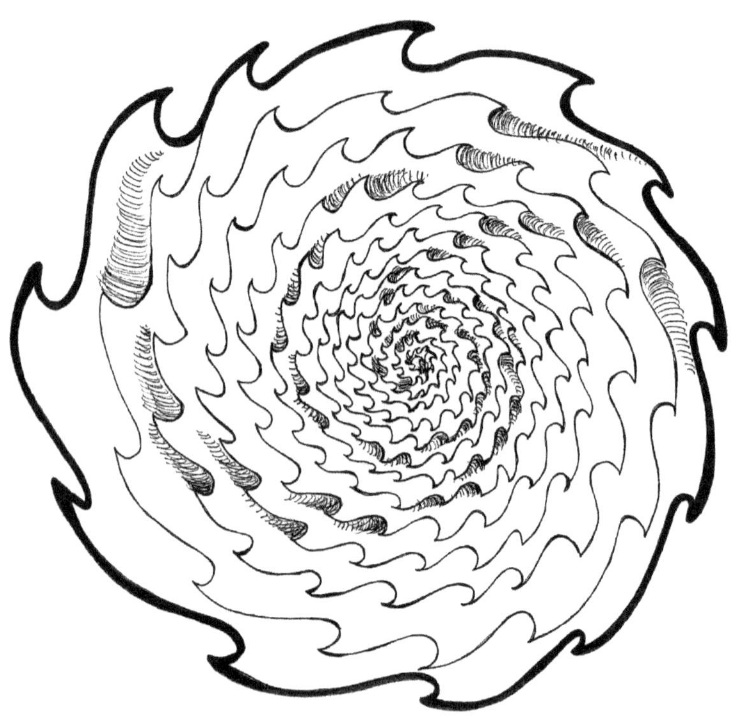

Moonlight

Little waves catch
the moonlight.
Procession leads us
to a horizon bright,
glowing
on the faces.
Day creeping into night.
Bridge the space
between us,
full moon
sand and sea.
Painting waves
like time worn faces.
Everlasting
motion
of moonlight
on the waves.

Sunshine

Unafraid to tell how we feel.
Guided on all sides,
keeping the current real.
Sundog streak across the sky,
into loves beckoning hand.
Feels good jamming in the band.
Palm trees in the fields,
old theaters dot main arteries.
Mountain ranges,
desert rampages.
Steel cars rattle by.
Stench and such.
AM/FM
Driving by at rapid speed.
Stretch our bones.
"Our way" highway.
Sundog follows a wandering eye.
Rails divide,
orchards abide.
Sing us up some sunshine.
Before our clouds collide.

{ 4 }

Spirit

Four Directions

Home of our heart.
Heart of our home.
We find love within the Great Mystery.
Deepening a bond
of spirit and life.
A great awakening
to love and bliss.
Sunlight pours
from our eyes.
Bathing us in radiance
and pure knowing.
All life is sacred.
A real man.
A real woman.
Returning together as one.

Moment

Hummingbird
shadow on the ground.
Looking up
to see her
already flown.
Her 'chirp' sounds
up
in the trees.
Her spirit
clings to me
praying on my knees.
Messenger of joy
that lights my
path to peace.
Knowing in a moment
this joy
has been released.

All My Relations

Deep in vision time.
Healing them as they dance.
Up the rope,
through the Tree.
Directly into the celestial
ceremony.
The tipi here on earth,
reflected above and below.
As it is.
Here and now.
Fulfilling the vision.
Healing the healer.
Making us strong.
The making of
all my relations.

Look At The Tree!

The
living
Tree
lives
in
me.
Patterns
drawn
in
the
earth.
By
the
feet
of
sun dancers.

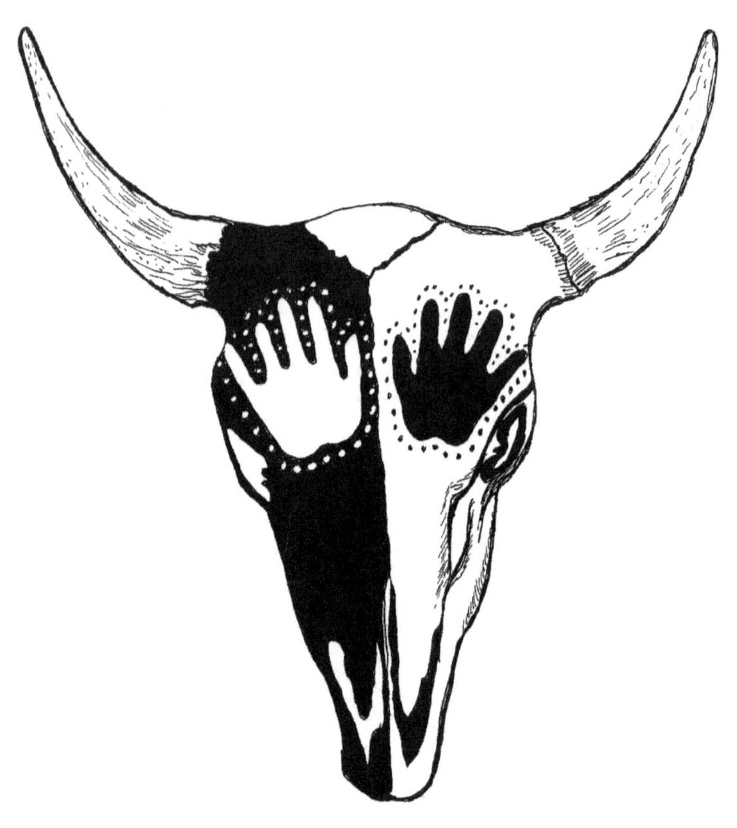

Blue Day

Profiles
in the
firelight.
All is dark
except for dancers
and the Tree.
Dancing
in the blue day.
By moon,
stars,
and milky way.
Our relatives
are drawing near.
Circles
around a
moonlit clearing.
Silhouettes
against the flame.
A star here
on earth
remains.

{ 5 }

Musings And Writings

I Was Pulled In

Excerpt from a poem written on a train from
Berlin to Prague.

I was pulled in,
called to by floating memories....
their hesitating departure.
Unconsciously I hear voices,
murmuring, shouting, crying.
Gasping for their last breath-
Before the death wall.
Within the torture chamber.
Before a dying, starving child.
Before a beaten comrade.
Before a burned body.
The breaths do not come easily today.
The breath in me
is the breath in those
forced to breathe
the breath of the torturer.
A breath of hatred,
I do not want to take in.

Wind circles in and out,
through the chambers of our hearts.
Flowing through the chambers
of hatred's victims.
Inside and outside the uniforms.
Ignorance and shame keeps many from feeling.
Remembering is too painful.
How can we put the circle of life back together
to stop the hatred?
Voices are heard by the millions
touched by war.
An....endless....stream....of....memory.
Tears in my eyes.
War stomps on my heart.
Caged spirits set free on the wind of time.
When will we be free?

ASH of
OBALIZATION
NAFTA
RE HUMAN POTENTIAL HAS BROUGHT US THUS FAR

In The Shadow (aka. Axis Of Evils)

It seems so endless. The constant weight of a machine on the back of Mama. We scatter at the impact of life being forced into death. Then we gather again to reconcile, to re-establish and renew strength. Sometimes I wonder who's getting stronger? Do we absorb the strength of the standing tree elders once they fall? Do the business suits gain strength by bulging bank accounts? There is an emptiness in the hearts of those who see dollar signs as they cruise through the forests. An emptiness learned. We are all taught this!

What I'm writing on right now. Post, percent, milled all the same. Consumed and forgotten. Sometimes I wish the blades would turn in on itself and be wreaked by it's own havoc. How easy it would be if the machine halted at the edge where humans justify and execute the job. If the machines had a better conscience than a reasoning human, the destruction wouldn't have gone this far.

What a plague we humans have created. What a dismal fate. As if war, death, ecocide, and constant exploitation were attractive and effective. Almost desired. Some sick sense of success. Who could ever be content in a bubble created from the money made from blatant death? To cruise the pavement in cool cars makes for a better outlook, but don't look too closely. The steel structures are cold and have no congratulations in store for the death dealers. Just another cold look. One giving and receiving a cold stare. Six feet under.

Oh! This world on the earth. The more I know, the more the truth hurts. Inside our landscapes, our souls are being desecrated by the life of earth's suffering all around. Yet, she always renews herself. Even if only a little shred or seed comes back. The more our souls are cut away along with these intense fabrics of life, the more raw I feel. Raw, like her clear cut face. Sometimes that feeling of immediacy comes over me as if the world on earth can come to a crashing halt at any moment. Because the pressure is too great. We know that this life is too precious to leave to the wayside. All our visions, hope, and dreams of what is to come. For us, we have a collection of years lived, years coming, and a new year always upon us.

The earth bears all our knowledge. So freely she gives to us all she knows. Hopefully we can take the time and listen to the constant rush and wind of knowledge that soars up this river canyon, and flies down on the backs of raindrops. This knowledge is embedded in the flesh of the deer we nourish our bodies with, and lies deep in the pools of water on earth.

We go through the workout to discover that all we need is the magic four letter word. L. O. V. E. The one basic concept that is constantly overlooked. What we love is what we are. Can we save our hearts from the machine minds of thoughtless, loveless humans?

So we live on the edges. Submersing ourselves in truth. Because living a lie is impossible once we've been there. Let truth guide our hearts, forever striving for a freedom that eludes us at every corner. We keep learning and re-learning that this freedom is not delivered on a silver platter. It burns in us. Deep from the roots of a people set free by truth.

This fire needs rekindling. Art needs to be made. Another day of truth leading the pack of riff-raff of resistance. A new way to live for today. The flow of Mama is undeniable. This heart beats.

How We Say Goodbye

Oh, how do we say goodbye to our loved ones? Sitting on the river bank as their spirits rise. Looking into the sky, the horizon is far away. Wondering about where they go into the beyond. Understanding only the feeling of the Great Mystery. Do we step off into the continuing plane of existence? Does the soul continue? Knowing that only the form has changed?

These things are fleeting. Rising away from thought as life sends us little reminders. The bugs buzzing. A deer slowly grazing nearby. Water surging on the bank. Road and air traffic snapping us to. Causing us to leave our daydream of the unknown future.

I know why I'm in love with life. It's sometimes confusing, painful, and just plain shocking! Some of the things I've seen. A slice of human nature unfolding every second we get to live. Often glorious moments of pure joy. When children show and remind us of the wild abandon of our youth. Checkered with times of loss, and near death experiences. The lightning quick changes of one's reality. How loss is only felt by the living. Great Mystery knows! The journey to the other side is unknowable.

Mother Jones said, "Pray for the dead, and fight like hell for the living." Yes ma'am! I'll add a prayer for the innocence of children, the patience of adults, and the shared wisdom of the elders. Keeping the memories of our dearly departed loved one's alive. Living a life full of rich and rewarding experiences. Cultivating gratitude and forgiveness. Standing up for the ones who have no voice or have been silenced. I want to live life to the fullest. Because, one day we won't be here anymore.

Rosalie Jones was born in Ventura, California in 1977. She took private art lessons from artist Kim Loucks until attending Ventura High School where she studied with Patti Post. Rosalie moved to Arcata, Ca. to study at Humboldt State University. She graduated with honors in 2001. Her Interdisciplinary major included Art, Women's Studies and Literature. Rosalie now lives with her husband of 22 years in the beautiful northern California mountains. Together they own and operate their business RXR Studios Research And Development. Some of Rosalie's creative work includes writing poetry, lyrics and music for their band RXR, illustrations, developing thematic paintings, and volunteering much of her time with the local Wintu tribe.

This is a statement about self confidence:

"YOU ARE ENOUGH! Written on all our mirrors at home. The self motivated artist has to keep finding and tending the creative fire within and believe in oneself. I Am Enough! is a daily mantra giving me the courage to stay creative and never give up on my artistic goals and dreams. Write it on all your mirrors too, because you are enough!"

Rosalie Jones

RXRSTUDIO.COM